Expecting

devotions for Advent

SCOTT HOEZEE

FAITH
ALIVE®
Christian Resources

Grand Rapids, Michigan

These devotions were originally published in 2001 by Faith Alive Christian Resources as part of the HomeLink series.

Expecting: Devotions for Advent, © 2010 by Faith Alive Christian Resources, 2850 Kalamazoo Ave. SE, Grand Rapids, Mich. 49560.

Library of Congress Cataloging-in-Publication Data
Hoezee, Scott, 1964-
  Expecting: devotions for Advent / Scott Hoezee.
    p. cm.
  ISBN 978-1-59255-541-3
  1. Advent—Prayers and devotions. I. Title.
  BV40.H64 2010
  242'.332—dc22

                                              2010028434

10 9 8 7 6 5 4 3 2

The Inevitable Surprise

"Therefore keep watch, because you do not know on what day your Lord will come."

Read Matthew 24:36-44

"The Son of Man will come when you do not expect him." That's what Jesus said long ago. The quirky thing is that these words are preceded by a lot of other words in which Jesus says that for sure he *will* be coming back and that, therefore, the disciples had to keep watch. But as the folk on Sesame Street like to say, "One of these things is not like the other!"

Most events in life that are "unexpected" are defined that way because the event came out of the blue. There had been no warning, no hint that this event was coming, and so no one was watching for it. The bombing of the Federal Building in Oklahoma City was unexpected—there had been no prior information that this was going to happen. No one was watching out for Timothy McVeigh or for a yellow truck that was riding suspiciously low on its axles.

On a happier note, a surprise visit from your favorite aunt who lives in New Zealand can also be unexpected. The doorbell rings, you go to the door assuming it's FedEx, only to discover Aunt Louise paying you an unannounced visit from halfway around the world. But suppose Aunt Louise had written you in advance to say, "Keep an eye out for me because I'm heading your way!" In that case, you would be watching for her. Even if she arrived at a time rather different than you had at first thought, you would still not call her arrival "unexpected."

So how can Jesus predict his return, order the disciples to keep watch, and still say that his return will be in any way "unexpected"? If we are honest, we may be able to locate the answer in our own hearts. Do you really expect Jesus to return? If you are a Christian, then you believe he will return. But do you really *expect* it?

Sometimes after a child is born, you may hear the new mother say, "I sure didn't expect this little guy to come into the world when he did! There we were, stuck in traffic on the interstate in the middle of a thunderstorm, and suddenly I went into labor!" Having a baby just then would be unexpected indeed, but at least the pregnant woman had known all along that a baby was coming—she'd even spent nine months getting ready for it by taking good care of herself. Not a day had gone by when she didn't do certain things, take certain vitamins, avoid certain foods and drinks, all because she was "expecting."

As we enter a new Advent season, it may be good to ask ourselves how often we reflect on the fact that this creation is "pregnant" with the new creation. If we are heeding Jesus' advice and watching very carefully, then only the exact calendar date will be unexpected. The event itself will be something we had been getting ready for all along.

Think or Journal
Has your expectation of Jesus' return influenced you recently? How?

Advent Wondering

God has chosen to make known among the Gentiles the glorious riches of this mystery, which is Christ in you, the hope of glory.

Read Colossians 1:24-2:5

What does your family do to prepare for Christmas? How do you mark the progression of Advent? Years ago my wife bought an Advent calendar for our children. Beginning on December 1 and continuing to December 25, the children would take turns sticking a little Velcro figure onto a manger scene each day. The figures included shepherds, magi, angels, animals, harps, trumpets, and, of course, Mary, Joseph, and baby Jesus. To the dismay of my older daughter, her little brother would sometimes place these items in odd spots. It was not at all unusual, some Decembers, to see a donkey soaring up in the stars over the stable and an angel being stepped on by a camel on the barn floor!

Perhaps you have your own Advent tradition by which you progressively check off the days leading up to the main event in Bethlehem. Family traditions are a wonderful way to mark the season, but perhaps we are sometimes stuck in our traditions. Maybe our thinking needs to be turned upside-down now and again so that we get startled into a fresh appreciation for what Paul calls "the glorious riches of this mystery." Just as my son flipped things around by making donkeys fly and angels lie, maybe we need to turn things over a bit in our own minds to ask some good questions about Advent.

The world may be content to cover up the wonders of this season with so much tinsel and wrapping paper. But we Christians need to be willing to probe a little deeper. A little holy puzzlement in Advent won't hurt us one bit. We should wonder, along with our children, what really went on. How could God's Son, whose glory fills the universe, manage to get squeezed into Mary's small womb? Was Jesus aware of where he was and what was happening to him? Once he was born, what did Jesus look like? Did he have his mother's eyes? Did it ever bother Joseph that Jesus did not resemble his side of the family at all? As Jesus grew up and learned things like how to hold his own cup when he drank, was he just *pretending* to learn? Or did he really not know things until someone taught him?

These questions merely scratch the surface of the glorious riches of the mystery that God kept hidden from ages past. "There's no such thing as a dumb question," people often say. The same applies to our Advent wondering. The questions we ask may very well help us get in touch with the profound mystery of Christmas—a mystery we cherish as "the hope of glory."

Think or Journal

Why do we spend four whole weeks observing Advent? What activity do you find the most helpful to prepare for Christmas?

Season's Greetings

"At that time people will see the Son of Man coming in clouds with great power and glory."

Read Mark 13:24-31

Have you received any Christmas cards yet? It's still pretty early in this holiday season, so it's possible that only a few have trickled into your mailbox. But maybe by the end of the month you will have received a tidy pile of cards. Some people place these cards in a holder shaped like a sleigh. Others arrange them on top of the piano. Still others tape them around a large doorframe somewhere in the house.

Every once in a while you may receive a card that strikes you as novel or quite clever. But for the most part the average Christmas greetings we get from family and friends are pretty predictable. Typically you see some kind of artsy picture of angels and shepherds or some fancy calligraphy presentation of Isaiah's words about the "Prince of Peace." This year's cards may be very similar to the ones you receive every other year. But that doesn't prevent people from sending them just the same. Each year, post offices in the United States and Canada sort and deliver millions of these cards, making December the single busiest month for mail carriers everywhere.

As far as I can tell, there's one traditional Advent reading that has never yet been pictured on a greeting card. It's found in Mark 13. The reason you won't find it in your mailbox is obvious: at Christmas we want the stars to twinkle, not to fall from their orbits! This is the time of the year when we want to see the gentle and serene *baby* Jesus lying in a manger. Who wants to decorate their mantel with a greeting card featuring the fierce Son of Man returning on clouds of glory to judge the world? Who wants to open a Christmas card and find a greeting that says, "Best Wishes for a Happy Outcome on Judgment Day"?

Still, as Christians we believe that ever since the day Jesus arrived on this earth, the entire cosmos has been that much closer to the final great Day. Referring to a fig tree, Jesus said, "As soon as its twigs get tender and its leaves come out, you know that summer is near" (Mark 13:28). So also our faith informs us that when the Son of God comes down to this earth to live, die, and be raised again, it is only a matter of time before he returns to complete his work. As we said on Sunday, the whole universe is pregnant with expectation. Jesus assures us that the new creation is "right at the door," ready to burst in, just like a baby ready to be born into the world. This is our real hope.

After all, if we can't celebrate our anticipation of Jesus' second coming with as much enthusiasm as we devote to his first, then all the greeting cards in the world will be completely meaningless.

Think or Journal
If you were to design your own Christmas card, what could you include as a reminder that Jesus is coming back?

All the Lonely People

"If this man were a prophet, he would know who is touching him and what kind of woman she is—that she is a sinner."

Read Luke 7:36-50

In yesterday's devotion, I predicted that you might end up with a tidy pile of Christmas cards later this month. But that will not be true for everyone. Maybe you do not have a close family or many friends. Perhaps reading yesterday's devotion was a painful reminder to you of just how lonely you are. In their poignant song "Eleanor Rigby," the Beatles repeatedly sing the chorus, "All the lonely people, where do they all come from? All the lonely people, where do they all belong?" The unhappy fact is that ours is a world chock-full of loneliness. For some people this holiday season deepens that sense of isolation.

Christmas has come to be touted as "family time." Happily, many families do manage to come together for holiday reunions that are genuinely enjoyable. But many others don't get together at all because there is simply too much bitterness between family members. They simply cannot all be under the same roof anymore. Still others manage to get through the gift exchange, but after everyone has gone home, Mom cries herself to sleep because she senses, better than anyone else, the deep tensions that lie just beneath the façade of togetherness.

Curiously, Jesus, whose birth and life we celebrate in Advent, spent almost his entire earthly ministry away from his family and in the company of lonely and outcast people. Sometimes he even turned his own family away to be with others who needed his loving presence more.

Today's story from Luke 7 is just one example of many in the Bible where Jesus touched and was touched by a person who lived on the lonesome fringes of society. This nameless woman who anointed Jesus' feet had not been invited to the dinner party that night. It is likely that she was never invited anywhere, since she was clearly a woman with a bad reputation. But that did not prevent Jesus from loving her, accepting her, and forgiving her. She was precisely the kind of person for whom Jesus came into this world in the first place.

If you plan to celebrate all or part of Advent and Christmas this year with family and friends, then you have good reason to rejoice and give thanks to God. But maybe your mailbox won't fill up with cards. Maybe your phone won't ring off the hook with invitations to parties. Maybe the most you can look forward to on Christmas Eve is a bowl of macaroni and cheese in front of the TV. But remember this: the Jesus whose birth we honor came for you too. You won't find Jesus only at loud and happy family get-togethers—you'll find him with you, wherever you are. That's why Jesus was born, because God so loved the world . . . because God so loved *you*.

Think or Journal
Are there people you could reach out to in this holiday season? How could you show the love of Jesus to them this year?

A Terrible Song

"[God] has brought down rulers from their thrones but has lifted up the humble. He has filled the hungry with good things but has sent the rich away empty."

Read Luke 1:46-55

Before the invention of recording devices, listening to music was a rare event. During Mozart's time, the only chance you would have to listen to one of his beautiful symphonies would be if you were lucky enough to hear some orchestra play it live. Muzak (music designed to *not* be listened to, like elevator music) would have been unthinkable in Mozart's day. Back then, if you were lucky enough to hear music being played, you *listened*.

But no longer. Even the grand carols of the Christian tradition have now been reduced to background noise in shopping malls. Shop at Walmart this month and you may very well hear "Silent Night," followed immediately by "Frosty the Snowman." Then, before you finish picking out which can of mixed nuts you want for next week's party, you may be treated to a medley weaving the notes of "Joy to the World" together with "Deck the Halls."

Today, in Luke 1, we bump up against an Advent song that widens our eyes and unstops our ears. Mary was an ordinary girl, but here she sings a most *extra*ordinary song! In Mary's Song we can hear the eerie combination of a teenager's

11

sweet voice and the words of terrible destruction. Somehow the angel's revelation that Mary would bear God's Son put this ordinary young girl in touch with a fundamental truth: God is the God of great reversals. As surely as the Lord exalted this humble girl, so also would those who are exalted in their own eyes be humbled. As surely as God would birth his Son smack into the midst of poverty, so also would those who exploit the poor of this world be impoverished.

Mary was quite correct. The Savior born in a barn is not always a welcome presence for those who live in castles. The innocent Jesus, who willingly allowed himself to be falsely accused of sin, is a thorn in the flesh for those who fancy themselves perfectly righteous without a Savior's help.

Mary's Song reminds us that Christmas is all about God's great reversal of everything. Our problem is that we have come to *expect* Jesus' birth in a stable—so much so that we forget that this bizarre entry into the world was just the first of a very long string of reversals.

We typically fail to listen to the background music that surrounds us. But Mary's Song in Luke 1 is one piece of music we need to listen to carefully. And as we hear Mary's sweet voice singing out these startling words, we should drop everything and learn.

Think or Journal

Compare a sampling of four or five of your favorite Christmas carols with Mary's Song. How do they stack up in capturing the wildness of God's daring plan as proclaimed in Luke 1?

Magnifying the Holy

"My soul glorifies the Lord and my spirit rejoices in God my Savior."

Read Luke 1:46-55

The computer revolution of the 1980s was made possible by a process known as *microminiaturization*. That nine-syllable mouthful is a pretty big word for something so tiny! It refers to the manufacturing of incredibly small microchips onto which ultra-small instruments are able to solder vast amounts of memory held by tiny circuits. The computer I used to write these devotions was run by a computer chip that was not much bigger than my thumbnail. It doesn't look very impressive if you examine it with the naked eye. But put that chip under a magnifying glass and the immensely complex series of circuits and micro-wires that snake around that wisp of silicon will blow your mind.

In order to clearly see something that is very small, you need to magnify it. Mary's Song has traditionally been called "The Magnificat" because, in the Latin version of Luke 1, Mary opens this quirk of a Christmas carol with the words "My soul *magnifies* the Lord!" But how can Mary (or any mere human being) magnify the God who fills the heavens with glory? How can someone as small as Mary make God any larger?

13

Yet Mary declares her desire to make God bigger, grander, easier to see. In a way, Mary is merely returning a favor: God lifted up lowly, ordinary Mary, magnifying her name and fame for all generations. So Mary, in turn, magnifies God, making God's character and glory more plain for all generations.

In Advent, as always, we are called to do the same. We shouldn't let our own smallness stand in the way of lifting God up ever higher. People should see God's grace and love in us. Through our witness to the Christ of Advent, we should help to make God large and plain and unmistakable for people to see.

Too often folks fancy *themselves* as this world's big shots. In the well-known song "New York, New York," Frank Sinatra croons that what he wants more than anything else is to wake up one day as "king of the world, top of the heap." That's a goal many people have. The problem with those who believe they're at the "top of the heap" is that they spend a lot of time looking *down* at all the "little people." But they seldom take time to look *up* at the God whose grandeur properly puts them in their place. If we can magnify God for such people, perhaps they too can come to love Jesus, who was exalted by becoming the top of a garbage heap called Golgotha. *That* is the God we need to magnify for the sake of those who, most days, miss seeing God altogether.

Think or Journal
How can you magnify the Lord this Advent season? How could you do that at work or in other places where God's presence doesn't always loom as large as it should?

Advent Spirit

"The Spirit of the Lord is on me, because he has anointed me to preach good news to the poor. He has sent me to proclaim freedom for the prisoners and recovery of sight for the blind, to release the oppressed, to proclaim the year of the Lord's favor."

Read Luke 1:51-52; 4:16-21

For the past several days we have thought about the way God reverses expectations. We've seen that God does not always start where we expect or work with the kind of people we would expect. Way back, at the dawn of the covenant, God wanted to raise up an entire nation of people out of whom the Messiah would one day emerge. So what did God do? He knocked on the tent flap of two senior citizens who had been unable to conceive a child, even in the flower of their youth. Later, the nation that wondrously emerged from Abraham and Sarah's offspring found itself in abject slavery and in desperate need of rescue. So what did God do? He called a stuttering and desperately shy man named Moses to take on the full force of the brutally powerful Pharaoh.

On and on the pattern repeats itself in Scripture—until, at long last, God sends Christ into the world. Consistent with God's usual way of doing things, that wondrous event occurs without any pomp or circumstance. No angel armed with a flaming sword comes knocking on Caesar's marble door. Instead, God skulks along one of history's back alleys and quietly slips a helpless infant into a manger. Later that baby grows into a man who is a chip off the old block. He delivers his first sermon on the theme of God's love for all the quiet underdogs of the world.

From there, Jesus goes on to cobble together a ragtag group of followers—mostly fishermen, a few despised tax collectors, other "sinners," even a few former prostitutes. The oppressed, the lowly, the simple, those held captive by poverty and racism: these are Jesus' kind of people.

Mostly, our society gets it wrong when it tries to depict what Jesus' Advent (coming) means. But one feature typical of the North American holiday season does ring with a faint echo of Jesus' mission. That feature is our focus on charities. For instance, throughout the holiday season, *The New York Times* puts the phrase "Remember the neediest" somewhere in the margins of almost every page.

It sometimes seems that our society focuses on charity during Advent in order to give folks in soup kitchens a "Merry Christmas." We're fine with leaving them in their poverty the rest of the year. But our goal as Christians is nowhere near that modest. We want the needy to have life abundant at all times. After all, the real Christ of Christmas is the one person who never had to be reminded to "remember the neediest." That's been God's way from the beginning.

Think or Journal
Think about some person or charitable group you have helped out or will help out this month. What will you do for this person or group during the rest of the year?

An Unwelcome Guest

"Repent, for the kingdom of heaven is near."
Read Matthew 3:1-12

In the last few years I have attended some pretty upscale pre-Christmas soirees. These parties are held in elegant old homes with oak-beamed ceilings, parquet floors covered with oriental rugs, and large fireplaces casting a warm amber glow. The food is as elegant as the surroundings—platters of steaming hors d'oeuvres, delicious cheeses, and eye-catching Christmas cookies.

These festive affairs contribute to the joy of the season. They draw us together in the love Christ has given us. Sometimes, though, I wonder what it would be like to have John the Baptist show up at one of these events. As all four gospels make clear, John was not exactly the Bible's most refined character! John's face was as rough-hewn as chiseled granite. His shaggy beard and unkempt hair perhaps contained remnants of yesterday's breakfast. And his demeanor quite effectively matched his appearance.

John was socially awkward. He was a bit too direct for most people's taste and didn't hold much respect for the "finer" things in life. At a Christmas party, I imagine John would slosh eggnog on the rug during an animated tirade. Not at all content with the usual party chatter, he would cut to the heart of it all. He'd toss out phrases like "Repent" and "Shape up" and "Woe to you" whenever he could. All in all, John the Baptist might be the center of attention, but he'd hardly be the life of the party. He'd more likely kill it instead.

At least, that's the John we meet in the gospels. But John always had a reason for his in-your-face attitude—to prepare the way for God's Christ. God was on the cusp of something new in the universe, and John was desperate to ensure that no one would miss out. If being a touch rude was what it would take to help people welcome the Messiah, then that is what he would be. After all, the Advent of the Christ is serious business—the most serious thing to come along since the original creation! It's not something to be treated lightly.

Because John unsettles our holiday cheer the same way he would likely unsettle our holiday party, he'd probably be an unwelcome guest. We don't put him onto our greeting cards. We don't include him in our Sunday school Christmas pageants. We don't hang "John the Baptist" or "Repent" ornaments on our trees. And yet—John appears in all four gospels, while the magi and the shepherds appear in just one gospel each. As Christians, we need John. If we don't heed his message, then we're not at all ready for Christmas—not even if all the party fixings are ready for the guests to arrive.

Think or Journal
Look back at John's words in Matthew 3. What things that John mentions could you do right now?

Moment of Truth

"I baptize you with water for repentance. But after me will come one who is more powerful than I, whose sandals I am not fit to carry. He will baptize you with the Holy Spirit and with fire. His winnowing fork is in his hand, and he will clear his threshing floor, gathering his wheat into the barn and burning up the chaff with unquenchable fire."

Read Matthew 3:1-12

Preacher Fred Craddock once told a story about a missionary family in China. Many years ago this family was under house arrest during the dark period when Communists were taking over. Finally the dreaded day came when a soldier banged on the front door and gave the family precisely two hours to pack up and prepare to be deported. They would be permitted, the soldier barked, to take with them exactly 200 pounds of possessions, not an ounce more.

So began two hours of frantic packing and family wrangling. What goes, what stays? What gets packed, and what gets abandoned in the quest for the prescribed 200-pound limit? The family had lived in China long enough to have accumulated a fair number of treasures. So they brought out the bathroom scale and began weighing one item after the next. What about these books? Valuable, but heavy.

19

What about this antique Chinese vase? Gotta take that. Well, maybe so, but the radio is brand-new.

On and on it went until finally they arrived at 200 pounds of stuff, just as the soldier returned. "Are you ready?" he asked.

"Yes," the father replied.

"And you weighed everything?"

"Yes, we did."

"Two hundred pounds?"

"On the dot, yes."

"Did you weigh the kids?"

"Um, no."

"Well, then, weigh the kids."

In a flash the books and the vase, the radio and the clothes became trash. Pure junk! The soldier's words were so shocking, so world-inverting, that the family's entire perspective was turned on its head. *Weigh the kids.* What had seemed valuable faded to unnecessary clutter in the face of the inestimable value of the children. The soldier's words created a startling moment of truth.

John the Baptist played a similar role in God's plan of salvation: to jolt people into new perspectives, new and better ways of assessing their lives. John wanted people to know that what they had always thought was valuable really wasn't—not in the light of God's coming Messiah. Compared to the supreme value of God's Son and what he came to do, most everything else we could possibly muster would be trash. In the light of John's moment of truth, let's leave the junk behind, so that we can once again embrace Jesus, our one true treasure.

Think or Journal

How does John's message hit you? What things in your life do you value more in the face of John's words? What do you value less?

The Advance Man

[John] came as a witness to testify concerning the light, so that through him all might believe. He himself was not the light; he came only as a witness to the light.

Read John 1:6-9

Years ago, the president of the United States was scheduled to give a speech in the auditorium just behind my son's preschool. I picked my son up at noon that day, and we took a picnic lunch to watch the busy preparations. Although the president's arrival was still several hours away, the place was crawling with police officers and people wearing fancy suits. Telltale wires snaking down the backs of their necks were connected to earpieces that kept them informed of what was going on.

Soon a metal detector was set up. Then roadside mailboxes were removed to prevent someone from planting a bomb in one. Eventually, sharpshooters wearing military jumpsuits and carrying long duffel bags climbed out of vans and made their way to the surrounding rooftops. Finally my son and I were politely asked to leave the area and to stand behind a new fence that had suddenly sprung up. Even more preparations for the president's arrival were invisible to us: hotel room walls were x-rayed, bomb-sniffing dogs checked every building where the president was going to be, and military aircraft silently patrolled the skies overhead to secure the airspace. The president's advance team did an amazing amount of work to prepare the way.

John the Baptist, as we've seen the last few days, was God's one-man advance team. It was John's vocation to prepare the world for the Christ. Through his blazing calls to repentance, John aimed to unveil what was really important in life. That way, when Jesus showed up with the grace needed to fix this world's deepest woes, people would be eager to receive him.

Have you ever had a repair person accidentally show up at your house? Maybe she got the wrong address or misread the house number. But suddenly you've got a plumber standing on your porch and carrying a toolbox, even though all the pipes and faucets in your house are in good working order. So what do you do? You tell her that she's made a mistake and that she's got the wrong house. You don't need her. On the other hand, if a pipe does burst, you urgently call the plumber, and you're eager to welcome her when she arrives. The welcome you offer (or not) depends on your situation, doesn't it?

John the Baptist knew that if Jesus simply showed up on the front porch of people's hearts, they might tell him to go away. So, as God's advance man, John revealed to them the spiritual equivalent of their burst pipes and leaky faucets. That way they might be glad, perhaps even overjoyed, to welcome Jesus when he arrived.

We are in the same situation today. If we hear, understand, and accept John's message, then we will fling open the front door of our lives to receive Jesus when he comes knocking. Because then we will know that Jesus is God's one and only Son, who alone can save us.

Think or Journal

Jesus came to repair broken hearts. In what way are our human hearts broken in the first place?

Christmas Fruit

"The man with two tunics should share with him who has none, and the one who has food should do the same. . . . Don't collect any more than you are required to. . . . Don't extort money and don't accuse people falsely—be content with your pay."

Read Luke 3:7-14

The Harry & David Company sends our family a lot of catalogs. The company sells gourmet foods, particularly cheeses, candies, and nuts. It's especially famous for its fruit. If you have ever eaten a Harry & David pear, then you know why the company is so famous. These are the juiciest, sweetest, most flavorful pears you'll ever bite into. Try one and you'll be reduced to eating like a toddler, with pear all over your face and juice dribbling down your chin! No wonder the Harry & David Company markets Christmas gift baskets of these and other delights, hoping that we'll want to share them with family and friends.

Luke records that John the Baptist poignantly called people to produce fruit consistent with a penitent heart. The people asked John what kind of fruit that would be, and John obliged them with some very interesting examples. Somewhat surprisingly, the fruit John was looking for appear to be quite ordinary. Be nice, he said; share your things; be honest; don't lie. Perhaps the people were expecting something more dramatic from this zany and dramatic preacher. Like the bestseller titled *All I Really Need to Know I Learned in Kindergarten*, John's advice ranks with what your kindergarten teacher might have told you once upon a time.

But maybe John's advice here is something like a Harry & David pear. From the outside it may look no different from the ordinary pears piled up in your supermarket's produce section. It's only when you bite into the pear that you discover that this one is far better than the others. In the same way, the fruit of repentance that Christians produce may seem similar to the good deeds performed by the local Rotary Club or Boy Scout troop. After all, many people in this world prize honesty, generosity, and a spirit of sharing. But somehow, when these are the fruit of repentance—when they are the result of a life that has been turned over to God and infused with his forgiving grace in Christ—they become that much juicier, sweeter, and richer. Then our fruit drips with the loving-kindness of God in ways that will last into eternity.

These Advent weeks we've been reflecting on the fact that the entire cosmos is expecting. The universe is pregnant with God's new creation just as Mary was pregnant with God's Son 2,000 years ago. But even while we wait, the Holy Spirit cultivates our lives, producing in us the righteous fruit of repentance—fruit for the world to delight in again and again, so that all may know the wonder of Christ, for whom John prepared the world.

Think or Journal
What "fruit of repentance" can you nurture in your life at work, at home, at school? Think of specific examples.

Funny Folks

"What should we do then?" the crowd asked.
Read Luke 3:1-14

Prophets were funny folks, and God asked them to do some very strange things. Nowadays, we sit in our comfortable church pews on Sundays and listen to the prophets' words and actions without sensing the spectacle they created at the time. Remember some of these prophets' antics?

Hosea married a prostitute.

Micah stripped naked and howled like a dog.

Jeremiah walked around for a long time with a yoke for oxen draped over his shoulders.

Jonah got puked out of a fish.

Ezekiel gave himself haircuts in the streets and then did funny things with the trimmings.

John the Baptist called himself the last Old Testament prophet. He certainly fit in with that motley crew. As Fred Craddock once pointed out, John was not just some vaguely antisocial hermit. He was a bizarre figure. He never cut his hair or beard. Never. He didn't merely sport a tidy little ponytail like some modern movie mogul—he had a ragged, shaggy hairdo and a beard like the one Tom Hanks grew in the movie *Cast Away*. John also ate bugs and wore animal hides. He was the kind of wild-eyed person who, if you ran into him in a deserted subway station, would make you go the other way as fast as you could.

Yet people came out in droves to see him. He became the most famous preacher of his day. John was so famous that many of his listeners concluded that *he* was the Christ. For many years after Jesus' resurrection, the apostles still bumped into people who believed that John was God's Messiah. All in all, John became amazingly famous, considering that he had but one sermon in his file. It went like this: "Repent! Repent! Repent, for the kingdom of God is at hand!"

The content of John's message, though simple, packed a huge wallop. It's a message we still need to hear, of course. John's original listeners were repeatedly cut to the heart. They cried out, "What can we do?" These days, unhappily, people mostly just cry out, "What can we get?"

John reminds us that what counts is not what we get. What really matters is what, by grace, we have already received: the gift of Christ. This is a gift to treasure, to be sure. But it is more than that; it is a gift that transforms us. And if we are not already living transformed lives, lives that make us as odd and as out-of-step with society as John himself, then we should seriously ask whether we've received this gift at all.

Think or Journal
Which question do you find yourself asking more during the holidays: "What can I do for God?" or "What will I get for Christmas?"

The Divine Delight

"The LORD your God is with you, he is mighty to save. He will take great delight in you, he will quiet you with his love, he will rejoice over you with singing."

Read Zephaniah 3:14-20

"Let me tell you about my grandchildren. . . ." Maybe you've seen that slogan on a bumper sticker or on a button pinned to someone's jacket. It's a line that makes us smile because we know that behind it lies a wealth of love, pride, and joy. But we also know that grandparents can get away with a lot more bragging about their grandkids than about their own children. Most of us get weary of parents who talk up their children. We extend grandparents a much bigger line of moral credit on such matters. When parents brag, you sense that they are calling attention to themselves as the ones responsible for their child's achievements. But when grandparents brag, it's all about the kids and the sheer delight those children bring to them, simply by being who they are.

In Psalm 90, the poet invokes a striking image by calling God a dwelling place, a home for his people. And like any good parent or grandparent, God loves it when the kids come home again. Combine that image with the lovely words found in Zephaniah 3, and a portrait of God as a grandparent emerges. It is clear that God delights in us.

29

Like a grandparent, God delights in us not because of what we do or achieve in life, but simply and solely because of who we are.

Zephaniah tells us that God loves to sing our praises. God is forever taking our pictures out of the divine wallet and showing us off to whomever will look and listen. We are accustomed to reading Bible passages that exhort us to give God all the praise and glory. Zephaniah 3 is a passage that delightfully turns the tables. Here we are promised a day when God will bring *us* praise and honor.

Christmas is all about God's love for us. But God's love always focuses on others as well. When someone loves us as much as God does, it's not an occasion for us to become arrogant and proud. It's an occasion for humble wonder. If we're honest with ourselves, we recognize that often we are not very lovable. We certainly don't deserve praise and honor from the supreme and holy Creator of the entire universe! But the wonder of Advent is that we receive this love anyway. We get it just by being the unique people God made us to be. That is reason enough, as C.S. Lewis once put it, to be "surprised by joy!"

Zephaniah predicted that the day would come when God would "take great delight in you" and "rejoice over you with singing" (3:17). That is God's way of saying to all who will hear, "Let me tell you about my grandchildren!"

Think or Journal
We often throw out the line "God is love." What does that really mean to you?

The Visited Planet

The earth is the Lord's, and everything in it, the world, and all who live in it.

Read Psalm 24

There's an interesting motif in C.S. Lewis's space trilogy. When the angels in heaven mention the planet Earth, a hush falls on them. Finally the silence is broken when someone remarks, "Ah, yes—that is the Visited Planet." Indeed, it's a hallmark claim of Advent that ours is the one planet in the universe where we know for sure that God came down in the flesh.

Planetarium shows can take viewers on a marvelous, three-dimensional tour of the universe. Most of them, including the one I saw recently, feature an imaginary ride through the solar system that takes us ever deeper into the galaxy. Typically we reach a point where we've traveled so far from Earth that our sun looks like just a pinprick of light, lost in the sea of thousands of other stars. Sometimes a little arrow points to our sun as the narrator observes dryly, "Sure doesn't look like much from here, does it?"

We know that space is vast, that stars are many, and that there are lots of planets whizzing around untold numbers of those stars. Yet, at Christmas, Christian people are bold enough to declare that, in the midst of all those vast interstellar stretches, our God is able to pick out our world. Ours is the Visited Planet. And we have this glorious distinction because God so loved this world that God's Son came here to bring us into his glory. No matter how far out into the reaches of space God "travels," God holds our world firmly in the divine gaze.

"The earth is the Lord's, and everything in it, the world, and all who live in it" (Ps. 24:1). The poet who wrote Psalm 24 could never have imagined how small Earth is compared to the rest of the cosmos. Maybe it would have shaken the psalmist up to know the truth revealed by contemporary astronomy. Still, it's not the size of the universe that makes the difference for us but the size of God's love for us. If your beloved daughter is spending a semester teaching in China, the distance between you cannot touch your love. You love her as much when she is in Beijing as when she's sitting right there on the sofa next to you. Advent celebrates the entrance into this world of "the King of glory." The love that brought about this glorious truth will never let us go. Ours is the Visited Planet. And so we will forever be the Lord's.

Think or Journal

Do you think that by visiting this one planet, Jesus was able to save the whole creation, including all of those other galaxies beyond our own?

Are You the One?

When John heard in prison what Christ was doing, he sent his disciples to ask him, "Are you the one who was to come, or should we expect someone else?"

Read Matthew 11:1-11

Today's passage seems profoundly disconnected from Advent. It's not about the baby Jesus. It's not about John the Baptist's Advent message of preparation. Instead, it describes an incident that happened after Herod had forced John into early retirement by throwing him into prison. Still, it has a lot to teach us about Advent and Christmas.

We have grown accustomed to keeping Jesus as the center of our attention at Christmas. We reflect on the fact that various people—including shepherds and magi—came to visit him. We see artistic renderings of the Bethlehem stable that place a halo over the head of baby Jesus or show some other kind of warm glow emanating from the cradle. We sing, "O come, let us adore him," expressing our desire to worship the One whom we naively assume immediately arrested the attention of the world.

But, of course, the true wonder of Advent lies precisely in the unspectacular way in which God the Son entered into our world. As we saw earlier this month, John the Baptist was a captivating, no-holds-barred, blazing firestorm of a preacher. He predicted that the Messiah would do all kinds of powerful, brilliant things. But the irony of the matter is that John ended up looking more dramatic than Jesus did!

Make no mistake. Jesus contained all the wonder and power John promised. But, as happens so often in history, God chose to reveal that power in gentle, quiet, humble ways. Jesus' kingdom grew on the mustard seed plan (see Matt. 13:31). That confused John—so much so that in Matthew 11 he dispatched a cadre of his disciples to ask Jesus if he was the One. Or should John be looking for someone else—someone better, still waiting in the wings?

That's a shocking question. How could John, of all people, have had doubts? Yet he did. In reply to John's question Jesus offered a gentle reponse. He sent John's disciples back to report on all that they had seen and heard about Jesus' quiet yet effective work among this world's most hurting and neglected people. That's all we have to go on too: the witness of what the disciples saw and heard and then wrote down for us to read. If John believed it then—and if you believe it now—it's not because any of this is so glaringly obvious or easy to grasp. It's because you have been given the gift of faith. Praise God for that truly precious gift!

Think or Journal

Do you ever wish you had been alive when Jesus walked this earth? Do you think it would have been easier to believe in him then compared to now?

The Person

For surely it is not angels [Jesus] helps, but Abraham's descendants. For this reason he had to be made like his brothers in every way, in order that he might become a merciful and faithful high priest in service to God, and that he might make atonement for the sins of the people.

Read Hebrews 2:14-18

Christmas is about an actual person. That may seem obvious to mention. But what does it really mean? For one thing, it means that our faith, our hope, and our joy are anchored to history. Think about it—no matter who you're dealing with, whether it's George Washington, Julius Caesar, or Mother Teresa of Calcutta, you need to think about that person in the context of the specific time during which he or she lived.

On the other hand, you can move a character who *isn't* real around history at will. For instance, in the first Superman comic books that came out in the 1930s, Superman was said to have landed in Kansas sometime in the early twentieth century. That way the Man of Steel would be an adult during the Great Depression—a time when people were sorely in need of superheroes. But in 1978, the writers of a full-length movie about Superman moved the time of his arrival to the 1950s. That way he would be an adult in the 1970s—just in time to chase errant nuclear missiles. It doesn't really matter when a make-believe character lived—what he or she stands for will work in almost any time.

But that's not true for real people. You can't retell the story of George Washington, but this time turn him into a twenty-first century figure. Washington has to stay in the eighteenth century, or else there is no story to tell! The same applies to Christmas. Our celebration takes place in the context of a definite spot on the chronological timeline of the planet. The story of Jesus is not some eternal truth that would have meaning whether or not it ever really happened. Jesus is too real, too specific for that.

There's more. Because Christmas is about a real person, Christmas is personal in the sense that we meet with some*one*, not some*thing*. Give thanks to God today that the Christ of Christmas is a real Somebody. Give thanks to God that Jesus is someone you'd recognize anywhere, once you got to know him. When Jesus appeared to a weeping Mary Magdalene on Easter morning, he only needed to say her name for her to recognize him. That's the joy of knowing Jesus as a true human being. And one day, when Jesus calls your name in the joy of the resurrection, you'll *know* him.

Think or Journal
In this season, when so many people talk about the "holiday spirit," what are some ways we can remind ourselves that Jesus is a real person?

It's Jesus!

". . . you are to give him the name Jesus, because he will save his people from their sins."
Read Matthew 1:18-21

One year my wife and I took our kids to the Radio City Music Hall "Christmas Spectacular" in New York. We sat through ninety minutes of nonstop production numbers, songs, and dances, in nine different acts. Santa Claus hosted the first eight. But just before the last act, Santa took off in his sleigh to make way for a lavish, living nativity scene. It had four real camels, a real donkey, five or so live sheep, and lots of colorful costumes. It had drama, pageantry, spectacle, music, and twinkling lights. The only thing it did *not* have was Jesus!

The scene lasted ten minutes and included a lot of narration by an unseen announcer. He talked on and on about someone who had once been born in Bethlehem—who lived and died, but who, for some reason, still influences lots of people even now, two millennia later. Yet nowhere in all of the words printed, projected, read, narrated, or sung was the name "Jesus" mentioned even once.

How strange! As we saw in yesterday's devotion, Christmas is about a *person*. Real persons have names. Christmas is not about an atmosphere or a spirit or an essence. It's about a real person who still lives. If all we're celebrating in Advent is an idea, a spirit, or a symbol, then it's hard to see how it really makes a difference. After all, we could spend our entire life thinking about the idea of love or the spirit of romance. But could such a concept ever remotely resemble what it's really like to be loved by another person? Because we're real flesh-and-blood human beings, ideas can take us only so far. Real people need more.

Some years ago I heard a lecture by a hospital chaplain. She told us about one little boy who had end-stage leukemia. In his last week of life the little boy suffered a lot of pain that seemed to cause hallucinations. Several times the boy saw a man passing by the doorway to his hospital room, causing him some alarm. His mother would reassure him that she was there and no one else. One afternoon, as the mother cradled her mortally ill child, the little boy cried out, "That man is back, Mommy!" The mother was about to reassure him once again, when suddenly his thin body relaxed. The boy looked her in the eye and, with a smile, said, "Oh, Mommy! It's Jesus! I have to go now." And with great peace, he died.

Christmas is about a person. On this all our hope depends. Christmas is about Someone in all his unique definiteness, Someone whom we can see and recognize and ultimately go with into the bright future he has secured for us. So look hard in this Advent season—pick out the face of the real person at the middle of it all. It's Jesus! Thanks be to God!

Think or Journal
Why do some people avoid the name of Jesus, even at a time of the year that's all about him?

This Bread

Whenever you eat this bread and drink this cup, you proclaim the Lord's death until he comes.

Read 1 Corinthians 11:23-26

Sometimes we can mix opposites and the result really turns out well. One good example is the delicious sauce that results from combining sweet and sour ingredients to make sweet and sour sauce, which originated in China and is now widespread in Western culture. Or think of oil and water—although they don't usually mix, skilled chefs have found ways to liven up a salad by combining olive oil and vinegar in an emulsion called vinaigrette.

But there are times when we'd just as soon avoid mixing opposites. Birth and death, for example. We'd prefer for them to stay far apart. Births are typically occasions for great joy. For many couples the anticipation builds for months until at long last they can see the little person who has been growing out of sight all this time. Precisely because a birth should be such a joyful event, we feel all the sadder when we hear the news of a stillbirth. A delivery room that should have echoed with the cries of the newborn and the laughter of adoring parents becomes very, very quiet instead.

Advent is a time when we anticipate a birth. Maybe that's why we feel even worse if we hear of a death during December. The pain of losing a loved one is as acute in the first few days of July as it would be in December. But if someone far from you dies on July 2, you seldom hear people react by saying, "Oh, what a shame! And so close to the Fourth of July!" Yet we do hear something like that about deaths in December: "And so close to Christmas!"

We resist allowing death to intrude on our celebration of Jesus' birth. That's why so many people prefer to let Christmas be both the beginning and the end of the story. Yet most churches will rightly celebrate the Lord's Supper at some point this month. Jesus' birth is far from the end of the story. An Advent celebration of communion reminds us of the reason Jesus was born as a real human being: to take our place in every way, including, ultimately, facing death.

Jesus is indeed "the reason for the season." These meditations have stressed that Jesus was a real person with a real name and a definite place in history. Jesus really is the reason *for* the season. But death is the reason *behind* the season. It's good that we proclaim Jesus' birth this month. Still, nowhere in the Bible does Jesus ask us to celebrate his birth. What he *did* command is that we keep on celebrating the supper commemorating his sacrifice and death. And so we do, Advent after Advent . . . until he comes again.

Think or Journal
Is it too grim or too morbid to stress Jesus' death also in Advent? Why is it important to do so?

Easter at Christmas

Christ has indeed been raised from the dead, the first-fruits of those who have fallen asleep.

Read 1 Corinthians 15:12-20

In yesterday's meditation we noted the necessary oddness of mixing up thoughts about Jesus' birth with thoughts about his death. Jesus was born to die. We celebrate the sacrificial nature of his death on the cross—a sacrifice that saves us. Proclaiming only Jesus' birth will never be enough for us. Perhaps that's why words about Jesus' birth occupy only a few verses in the gospels, whereas all four devote the bulk of their concluding chapters to his death.

But Christians need one more piece of good news as well: Jesus' resurrection from the dead on Easter morning. Belief in that cosmos-shattering event is the true dividing line between people of faith and everyone else. It requires very little faith to believe that Jesus was born one day and died on another day. But to believe that Jesus triumphed over death—that's another story.

Consider the way newscasters talk about Christmas and Good Friday. On Christmas Eve Katie Couric might say, "Tonight Christians around the world remember the birth of Jesus." Similarly, next spring, Brian Williams might say something like, "This afternoon the pope led worshipers in

Rome in a commemoration of the day Jesus died." But a couple of days later, when Easter rolls around, newscasters begin to hedge a bit, saying things like, "Today Christian believers mark the day when Jesus *allegedly* rose from the dead."

Suddenly people start throwing in wiggle words, qualifiers, phrases to convey that, unlike birth and death, resurrections are controversial and not easily believed by all. But Paul writes in 1 Corinthians 15 that if Christ is not raised, then our faith is futile, silly, a dead end. In these meditations we recall the Advent reminder that because of Jesus' birth, death, *and* resurrection, the cosmos is pregnant with the future hope of the New Creation. We're expecting! But the cosmic womb is empty if Jesus just lived and died like everyone else.

If right now, on this Advent day, you believe the cosmos is expecting Jesus' return in glory, then that's because you know Christ Jesus is raised from the dead. He's the firstfruits, the sneak preview, for all who follow him in faith. None of us was ever born the way Jesus was born. But we will all be raised like him! So this month we should be able to say "Merry Christmas" and "Happy Easter" in the very same breath!

Think or Journal
Christmas cookies and Easter eggs do not generally share the same buffet table. Maybe they should. Why?

Things Fall Apart

"But you, Bethlehem Ephrathah, though you are small among the clans of Judah, out of you will come for me one who will be ruler over Israel, whose origins are from of old, from ancient times."

Read Micah 5:1-5

As I wrote this meditation, things in the Middle East were about as bad as they had ever been in my lifetime. In the previous six months, a number of traditional Christian observances and worship services in Jerusalem and Bethlehem had been canceled due to security concerns. We may call the region the "Holy Land," but it has often been the setting for far too many unholy events.

In his poem "The Second Coming," William Butler Yeats captures something of this combination of holy and unholy in a world intent on rattling itself apart in hatred and terror. Perhaps the reason why this poem has been quoted so often in recent years is that it describes our world regrettably well. Already in 1920, well before most of the twentieth century's horrors took place, Yeats wrote, "Things fall apart; the centre cannot hold." And, fearing that some form of totalitarianism would soon take over the world, he concludes the poem with this question: "What rough beast . . . / Slouches toward Bethlehem to be born?"

Yeats and the Old Testament prophet Micah had some things in common. They both lived in troubling times of chaos. They both looked toward Bethlehem for some new revelation. Yeats, however, feared the advent of a nightmare. Micah promised the advent of all hope. Micah held out the promise of the Anointed One of God, despite the fact that, spiritually speaking, God's people were getting exactly what they deserved at the hands of the Babylonians. Nevertheless, Micah promised that God would be faithful to Israel despite Israel's sorry record of unfaithfulness to God. God would keep the ancient promise to David and would raise up a new, eternal leader for God's people. This leader would emerge from the backwaters of Israel—David's hometown of Bethlehem.

As a traditional carol puts it, "the hopes and fears of all the years" would come together in Bethlehem's stable. In many ways, it is an unhappy indication of the state of our world that the Bethlehem of today is ringed by guns, awash in a sea of violence. Now, as ever before, Bethlehem contains as many fears as it carries hopes. Things often do fall apart today, especially in the places where Jesus walked. But as Micah predicted, Jesus is the one who can lead his people "in the majesty of the name of the LORD his God" (Mic. 5:4). We have confidence that Jesus is not undone by whatever makes our world fall apart. In Christ, whose Advent we now celebrate, this world's hopes and fears can still meet, can still come together, and can still lead to the shalom of God. That's because, as Micah predicted, the child of Bethlehem *is* our peace—now and always.

Think or Journal
What things in our world make you afraid? Should we try to keep unhappy thoughts far from us during Advent and Christmas? Explain.

The Highway

"In the desert prepare the way for the LORD; make straight in the wilderness a highway for our God. Every valley shall be raised up, every mountain and hill made low; the rough ground shall become level, the rugged places a plain."

Read Isaiah 40:1-11

North Americans encounter a lot of travel metaphors. The Internet is the "information superhighway." The people at Microsoft used to tout their products with the slogan "Where Do You Want to Go Today?" We like to go places, and we like to get there fast. Today's highways allow us to do just that. To encourage us to use them, our highways include guardrails, reflectors, streetlights, emergency call boxes, and other important safety features.

The highways of the ancient world allowed for faster travel as well. But they were far from safe. In fact, highways through the wilderness were downright dangerous. Travelers risked being attacked by wild animals. They were vulnerable to assault by robbers. And they endured the threat of being overcome by the desert's intense sunlight and heat. That's why, throughout the Bible, the desert is a symbol for all that's gone wrong with our world because of sin.

That's also why Isaiah 40 is such a lovely chapter. Isaiah begins by promising that God is going to build a highway into this world—a safe and secure highway that will lead to peace. Better yet, a highway that goes straight through the wilderness. The very deserts of life, which are otherwise so dangerous and so fraught with sin and evil, will, by God's grace, become safe and secure.

The fact that God has built a safe highway for us in an otherwise perilous world was a source of real comfort for the people of Jerusalem. But it should be no less comforting for people in Toronto, Los Angeles, New York, or Omaha. In all of those places, we have reason to feel comforted. Why? Because God's Son began the work of building a "highway for our God" right through the desert of our lives.

That comfort also presents us with a challenge. We need to extend God's holy highway of love. We need to build it through the AIDS ward and the inner city. We need to build it through the back alleys ruled by street gangs and through nursing homes filled with despair. We need to build it through the lives of people who are mere outer shells of what they once were—people who were once vibrant and full of dreams but are now beaten down and hollowed out.

If Advent still has a message of comfort for us today, then it must come to these places. Because our great God in Christ still wants us to speak tenderly to the afflicted of this world—and not only at Christmas. We should keep proclaiming that message until every valley has indeed been exalted and every rough place smoothed out into a safe place for all God's people to dwell.

Think or Journal
What does the word comfort *mean in this passage? How is it different from the false comforts that many people seek today?*

God's Silent Partner

When Joseph woke up, he did what the angel of the Lord had commanded him and took Mary home as his wife.

Read Matthew 1:18-25

We may call the Christmas season a season of serenity, but it's actually pretty noisy. Preachers have lots to say on the subject of Jesus' Advent on this earth. Most of us can't wait to sing our favorite carols again and again. The malls are awash in Muzak. Concert halls across North America echo with the sound of Handel's *Messiah*. And the ringing of the Salvation Army's omnipresent bells fills in the auditory blanks on street corners.

Even the Bible passages we read at this time of year are filled with sounds. John the Baptist shouts, angels sing, shepherds and magi chatter curiously to one another, and Mary delivers her famous "Magnificat." But one character in the Christmas drama never utters a syllable. His name is Joseph. Nowhere does the Bible record a single word he said. Not one. Joseph forms the still, silent center to a story filled with words. Joseph speaks loudly, but only through his actions.

Matthew does not say much about Joseph except to note that he was a "righteous man" (1:19). Joseph wanted to do the right thing in honor of the God he served. The twist in this story is that God had different ideas about what the

47

right thing to do really was. Joseph had in mind to divorce Mary on the grounds of her seeming infidelity. But God told Joseph to stick with her, since Mary had not sinned. It was hard enough for Joseph to believe this, but he certainly knew that no one else would buy the story that Mary had conceived through the power of the Holy Spirit.

Joseph would simply have to bear the inevitable snide comments in silence. For the greater good, Joseph, a righteous man, would have to allow his own reputation to suffer. People would conclude that he was staying with a sinful woman who had run around on him before their wedding. Or they could privately snicker at Joseph's own impatience in not waiting for his wedding night. Either way, Joseph had to follow God's idea of the righteous thing to do, not his own.

That he did not protest God's command is a clear sign of how willing Joseph was to learn from God. Joseph said precisely nothing! As Ecclesiastes observes, there is "a time to be silent and a time to speak" (3:7). Sometimes we honor God best by simply accepting and trusting in silence God's own peculiar way of doing things.

In this Advent season there's much to say. But there's also plenty of mystery to ponder in obedient silence. On this last Sunday of Advent, let's take some time just to be quiet and meditate on the holy, righteous, and surprising things God has done.

Think or Journal
Do you think that Joseph ever told others what the angel had told him in his dream? Why or why not?

Note: Depending on which day of the week Christmas falls during the year you are using these devotions, you may not need to use all of the devotions that follow.

Have Fun

"John came neither eating nor drinking, and they say, 'He has a demon.' The Son of Man came eating and drinking, and they say, 'Here is a glutton and a drunkard, a friend of tax collectors and "sinners."' But wisdom is proved right by her actions."

Read Matthew 9:14-15; 11:16-19

C hristmas is a time for celebration. Yet we have a hard time imagining Jesus having a good time at our annual parties. Philip Yancey notes that many of the actors who play the part of Jesus in movies about his life portray him as a flat, emotionless character. The eyes are glassy, the manner serene, the voice monotone. Yet the actual Jesus who emerges from the gospels was someone people enjoyed being around. He was not necessarily the "life of the party." But at the very least he was popular enough to receive lots of invitations to parties.

People liked being around Jesus. And Jesus himself enjoyed eating a fine meal in the company of his hosts and the other guests. In fact, Matthew 11 records that Jesus was such a frequent guest at parties that his enemies found it possible to deride him as a glutton and a drunk! Neither charge was true, of course. But no one would have said those things about Jesus had he acted like a sourpuss or a loner.

Why is it important for us to keep this feature of Jesus' personality in mind? Because it reminds us that what we celebrate this season deserves all the joy, happiness, and fellowship we can muster. It also reminds us that as children of God, re-created in God's image through Christ, it makes sense for us to be exuberant folks too. We should be the kind of people others like to be around.

We often forget that. We get uptight. We become judgmental. We worry that by having too good a time in the company of non-Christians we'll not be able to provide a convincing witness to the gospel.

Remember that Jesus was not born smack into the middle of this world so that he could hang back from other people. Jesus came to engage this world, starting with the very people the religious elite tried so hard to avoid. Jesus did not come to put people off with a lifestyle that shunned pleasure and joy. He came to celebrate what is best about life, even as he consistently pointed people to the even better ways of God's kingdom. We can learn much from this aspect of God's incarnation as we prepare to join all God's people in the ultimate dinner party—the wedding feast of the Lamb.

Think or Journal
When you picture Jesus, what does he look like? Is he usually smiling?

Gifts

For the grace of God that brings salvation has appeared to all.

Read Titus 2:11-14

It can be a bit of a cliché to say that we give gifts in honor of Jesus, the greatest gift of all. That could easily become a pious excuse for excesses of greed and overspending. In that case, we are using the idea of Jesus as a gift in entirely the wrong way. But we cannot deny that Jesus truly *is* the greatest gift the world has ever seen. In Jesus we receive our lives back as a free, unexpected, unwarranted gift of grace.

This is one present you must not simply pack away and forget about once Christmas is over for the year. The gift of grace is so completely transforming that, once you unwrap it, it shapes you every day. As Paul writes to Titus, this gift gives us the power and the confidence to say no to a worldly way of life and yes to the kingdom lifestyle that Jesus taught.

This is also a present we can use right away, unlike that new bathing suit you may have received last Christmas. For that, you had to wait for the warm weather to come before you could use it. Months later, you had to hunt your Christmas present down so you could finally use it.

The gift of Jesus is not like that at all. According to Paul, it's a gift "in this present age" (Titus 2:12). We can use it immediately, and it will never go out of style or season. As Christians we believe that the entire universe is pregnant with divine possibilities. We're expecting! In verse 11, Paul points out that Jesus has already come. In verse 13, he declares that Jesus is also coming again. In between these Advents of Jesus, we live gracious lives that show evidence of the grace we have received.

This week gifts will be exchanged in many households. Lots of parents will fix their children in a direct gaze and say, "Jimmy, what do you say to Grandpa and Grandma?" "Thank you" is obviously the intended response. For most of the gifts we will get this Christmas, "thank you" will be sufficient. But when the gift in question is the living Son of God who died and rose for us . . . well, mere words will never be enough. Therefore we keep on living for Christ and to the glory of God so we can *show* ourselves to be a people "eager to do what is good" (Titus 2:14).

Think or Journal
How, in your daily living, have you said thank you to God for the gift of Jesus?

He Gave Himself

Jesus Christ . . . gave himself for us to redeem us from all wickedness and to purify for himself a people that are his very own, eager to do what is good.

Read Titus 2:11-14

Yesterday we thought a bit about our gift-giving tradition and its connection to Jesus as God's ultimate gift to us. Today we read the same passage from Titus to dive a bit deeper into this theme. In verse 14, Paul catches the enormity of the deepest meaning of Christmas with the simple phrase "[Jesus Christ] gave himself for us."

We often hear that the best presents are the ones that are homemade. When the candleholder for Grandpa doesn't turn out as planned, Mom reassures her disappointed child, "Honey, what matters most is that you made it yourself. Grandpa will be so happy to see the love you put into it. That's the best present of all!" We tend to particularly prize gifts that are endowed with love, effort, and time. We feel like we are receiving something of the giver in the gift.

But what if the gift we receive contains not just a portion of that person's love but the entirety of that person? If someone were to give me a new watch, I would be grateful. If she were to give me a piece of pottery made with her own hands, it would mean even more to me. And if someone were to donate a healthy kidney when I needed one,

I'd be speechless with thanks. But if someone were to lay down his or her life to spare mine, no amount of thanks nor any act of service could repay the gift.

That's the gift Jesus gave. Jesus gave *himself* for us—not just a part, but his whole self. Our only appropriate response to his gift is to live in ways that are consistent with Jesus' own fierce desire to make this world a better place. That's why Jesus laid down his life for us in the first place.

Sometimes people talk about catching "the Christmas spirit." They may imagine some vague mood of upbeat generosity like that experienced by old Ebenezer Scrooge in the famous Dickens story or by the nasty Grinch in the Dr. Seuss tale. Such transformations of heart and mind make for nice stories. But do you know of any real person whose life was genuinely and permanently turned around by the "spirit of Christmas"? I don't. Most of the grumpy people I know are just as grumpy and hard to like after Christmas as they were before.

On the other hand, I do know people whose hearts changed because they came to understand that Jesus gave himself for them. By Valentine's Day we may have a hard time remembering what we got for Christmas. But there's one gift we must never, ever forget: the Son of God who gave himself for us.

Think or Journal
Jesus gave himself for us. And long before he got to the cross, he gave up many other things. What are some of the things Jesus gave up for our salvation?

Advent Camping

The Word became flesh and made his dwelling among us.

Read John 1:14-18

Those of us who don't *dream* of a white Christmas—because we typically experience one—don't usually associate Christmas with camping trips. Someone might give us a new tent or camp stove for Christmas. But that would be one of the gifts we'd store away for later. And even those who do have a warm, sunny, green Christmas are unlikely to spend the holiday in a tent.

John 1:14 is a shattering and famous text. It is the incarnation of Jesus in a nutshell. What we sometimes miss, especially in current translations, is the camping metaphor that lies at the heart of this verse. Literally translated, this verse says, "The Word became meat and pitched his tent among us." Both images are a little crude. The Son of God became meat! The Son of God set up headquarters among us in nothing more than some moth-eaten old tent! How can that be? And yet it is precisely this kind of shock John wants us to experience.

The camping image is particularly vital. It ties in directly with the Old Testament experience of having God live in the midst of Israel by dwelling inside the tabernacle, the tent that the Israelites toted with them from place to place after their exodus from Egypt. The mystery of ancient Israel was that the God of the galaxies, the God whose power could not even be described or contained, actually came down and lived in a tent of wood and cloth.

Now God's Son has come here in no more than a "tent" of human flesh and blood. How can it be that all God's glory and power, all his grace and truth, get sewn up inside such an ordinary body? We cannot answer a question so profound. But recalling that in Christ this really did happen can refresh for us the wonder of Advent.

God's holy and mighty Word camped out among us. God was no more "at home" on this earth than we are when we're camped far away from the normal conveniences of our home. The dusty streets of Palestine were not the glorious precincts of heaven—not by a long shot! But Jesus came here and pitched his tent among us because in the long run, this trip would be worth it. In a tent of flesh, God's Word opened up a way for all of us to join Jesus forever in the glories of God's eternal presence.

Think or Journal
Few people in the Old Testament were looking for God's Messiah to become human and take a camping trip. What do you think they had been looking for?

With a Beginning Like That . . .

[Mary] gave birth to her firstborn, a son. She wrapped him in cloths and placed him in a manger, because there was no room for them in the inn.

Read Luke 2:6-7

"With a beginning like that, she never had a chance!" That's the kind of thing you might hear people say when they hear the life story of a convicted criminal. When we discover that a certain thief, drug dealer, or murderer grew up in a broken environment, we're not surprised that this person was headed for trouble. Or we may worry that such a future is inevitable when we hear of a child born under a highway overpass in the company of drunks and heroin addicts—a child swaddled in dirty rags and laid in a Styrofoam beer cooler for a cradle. "With a beginning like that. . . ."

By now you can see where I'm going: straight to the Bethlehem stable. We've seen so many pretty pictures painted of this scene that we tend to forget its sad tawdriness. Our favorite Christmas carols have us crooning lines like "Once in royal David's city stood a lowly cattle shed." But we put these words to such lovely music that even the lowly shed gets elevated. We talk about Jesus' birth in the stable with such lyrical voices and poetic stanzas that we block from sight what it was really like.

We sing about oxen "lowing," but we don't sing about the other things cattle do in a barn. We sing about the stars in the sky shining down on Jesus' sweet face, but we never mention that through the same cracks that let starlight in could come drenching rain and dew. It's easy to imagine that the folks back then who heard about Jesus' lowly birth might have shaken their heads and said, "Oh! How can he possibly amount to anything with a beginning like that?"

It's not just historical accuracy that should lead us to catch an acrid whiff of the stable on Christmas Eve. Getting our noses rubbed in Jesus' sad beginning in life helps to bring us more of the gospel's good news. No matter what your situation is this day before Christmas, Jesus understands it. Christmas can be a very painful season for many. Maybe a loved one has died since last Christmas. The pain you feel over the absence is so raw you feel like you can hardly breathe. Maybe you've lost your job and you're terrified about how to provide for your family.

But Jesus understands. Look again with fresh eyes at the tragedy of Jesus' birth. With a beginning like that, Jesus is perfectly positioned to understand our hurts. After all, Christmas is not first of all about the happy people in the world. Christmas happened precisely to help, comfort, and save all the unhappy people. That's why tonight is such a *holy night*. It leaves no one out. Thanks be to God!

Think or Journal
Christmas cannot magically make sad people happy. But how can Jesus' birth help this world's down-and-out folks?

In Perspective

In those days Caesar Augustus issued a decree that a census should be taken of the entire Roman world. (This was the first census that took place while Quirinius was governor of Syria.) And everyone went to his own town to register. So Joseph also went up from the town of Nazareth in Galilee to Judea, to Bethlehem the town of David.

Read Luke 2:1-20

Every year, untold numbers of children around the world struggle to wrap their tongues around the names "Caesar Augustus" and "Quirinius" in Christmas programs. We've grown so accustomed to the inclusion of these names in the traditional Christmas story that we don't bat an eye unless a child really messes them up. We easily miss the real humor and irony of the way Luke uses them in order to take us on a surprising journey.

The trip begins with Caesar Augustus. On that first Christmas Day he was the most famous man in the world. Augustus was at the top of the heap. But then Luke climbs down the ladder of fame. He introduces us next to Quirinius, the Syrian governor. Then we plummet even further down the social scale to meet up with a nobody named Joseph. He's from Nazareth in Galilee. That's today's equivalent of being from Hicksville or the boonies—as far from the world's power centers as it's possible to get. But if you thought Nazareth was a small, backwater town, look where Luke takes us next. To a cattle barn in Bethlehem!

Luke takes us on a Christmas journey from the heights of power at Caesar's extravagant palace in Rome to a straw-strewn stable in Bethlehem. His point? He wants us to delight in the humorous irony of God's way of doing things. The most powerful events in the cosmos do *not* occur in the rarified air where the world's "beautiful people" live. But that point is lost on most people.

I live in a city that has a lot of churches. Every Sunday, in the congregations scattered throughout the area, wonderful things happen: lives are changed, babies are baptized, young people profess their faith, the Lord's Supper is celebrated in all its sublime mystery, and God's truths are proclaimed by gifted preachers. But the world doesn't notice that one little bit! Church work and worship rarely generate headlines. By way of contrast, when Tom Hanks visited the area while shooting a movie, his presence was front-page news the whole week. Here at last was a sliver of Hollywood in our own backyard. We received a visit from one of the world's "beautiful people." Wow! Everybody knew about it.

Our world is forever looking in the wrong direction. While all eyes were focused on Augustus and Quirinius, God was busily working behind everybody's back. Even today, while the world watches all the wrong people in all the wrong places, God is quietly doing wonderful things to bring the "peace on earth" of which Jesus' birth was just a sneak preview.

Christmas is about looking in the right direction. So when we wish one another "Merry Christmas" today, let that remind us of where we should look to find God hard at work.

Think or Journal
Even on this Christmas Day, what tempts you to look for God in the wrong direction?

Now Dismiss Us . . .

"My eyes have seen your salvation, which you have prepared in the sight of all people, a light for revelation to the Gentiles and for glory to your people Israel."

Read Luke 2:22-35

Traditionally the Sunday after Christmas is a time to think about the events surrounding Jesus' infancy, even as we prepare to pivot toward Epiphany on January 6. After Epiphany we move on to look at the adult ministry of Jesus. The Bible tells us very little about Jesus' life between his birth and his baptism many years later. The longest single story is the one we read today about the presentation of Jesus at the temple forty days after his birth. Although Mary and Joseph followed the prescribed rules for this event, it's not surprising that it didn't exactly happen by the book.

The normal events of the liturgy were interrupted when an ancient-looking man shuffled up and asked to hold the baby. Mary must have hesitated. Those of you who are parents remember what it's like with your first child. You treat her like an eggshell. You're afraid that if you hold her the wrong way, she'll break. I remember driving my newborn daughter home from the hospital. I turned each corner ever so gingerly and winced each time we hit even the smallest pothole. So Mary must have worried about handing her precious little baby son over to a doddering old man. But hand him over she did.

Although glazed over by cataracts, the old man's eyes seemed to see farther than anyone else's. Simeon peered into Jesus' face even as the infant tugged at and played with the old man's beard. Simeon was peering down into a deep well of history, seeing not just a baby but the salvation of God. Outrageous things poured from the old man's trembling lips. He called Jesus a "light for revelation to the Gentiles and for glory to . . . Israel." Not the kind of thing we'd expect someone to say when cooing over a baby!

Simeon had somehow known for a long time that he'd live to see God's Christ. Luke tells us that the Holy Spirit had tipped him off. What Simeon may not have known was that the Messiah he'd eventually behold would be an infant too weak to even hold up his own head!

But when Simeon saw God's Son in this helpless state, he realized something marvelous. If God had to go to these lengths to establish salvation, then salvation must be a gift of grace indeed. And in that realization, Simeon received all the consolation anyone could ever want. To see what Simeon saw requires the eyes of faith—eyes that are able to recognize in that drooling, head-lolling, cooing little baby boy the salvation that came to this world as God's surprising gift.

Mary probably worried that Simeon would drop her precious baby. But Simeon knew there was no danger of that. His eyes of faith showed him that although he was holding the infant Jesus, it was actually Jesus who had Simeon, and the whole world, in *his* hands!

Think or Journal

What do you think Mary thought about Simeon's words? Would she have expected them? Would she have been taken aback?